# SEARCHING ON LOCATION:
## Planning a Research Trip

· Anne Ross Balhuizen ·

P.O. Box 476
Salt Lake City, UT 84110

Balhuizen, Anne Ross.
   Searching on location : planning a research trip / Anne Ross
Balhuizen.
       p.    cm.
   Includes bibliography.
   ISBN 0-916489-43-4
   1. Genealogy.    I. Title.
CS9.B35   1992
929'  .1 – dc20                                        92-3207
                                                          CIP

Robert J. Welsh, Managing Editor
Design and Production by Robb Barr

First printing 1992
10 9 8 7 6 5 4 3 2 1

Printed in the United States of America

# CONTENTS

# PREFACE

There is a certain value in approaching a research trip as a special activity separate from local ventures into libraries and archives. This book will serve as a guide for the person who wants to make maximum use of his or her time, money, and energy in a specific quest for family history.

Although it is divided into areas of interest, the book should be approached as a whole, since suggestions for one area may be applied to another. I have tried to call attention to information in other chapters. In some cases I have repeated material that was critical, but it still will be wise to use this as a total guidebook; it is not a series of unrelated topics.

The reader also is urged to make full use of reference books. A guidebook is just that—a guide. It does not substitute for source books with their in-depth treatment of material. The bibliography will direct you to some references. Any good genealogical section of a library should offer a selection of books that will give you the necessary skills to have a rewarding research trip experience.

As a reader of this guide you will be starting on a real adventure in genealogy. May you be successful in discovering your past.

Anne Ross Balhuizen has more than fifteen years of experience as a genealogical researcher. She has lectured, taught workshops, and for six years was a columnist for the "Kansas City Genealogist." In 1980 she established the Cumberland Gap Study Group, specializing in research in Virginia, North Carolina, Tennessee, and Kentucky. Much of the material she presents in this book is drawn from her discussions with others in that group about their experiences.

Mrs. Balhuizen holds a degree in psychology and has done graduate work in archaeology and ancient history. In addition to writing for non-genealogical publications, she has recently worked as a contract fiber artist for Hallmark Cards, Inc.

She is married to a physician and has two children and four grandchildren. Mrs. Balhuizen lives in Kansas City, Missouri.

## ACKNOWLEDGMENTS

I owe much to all those who have been so gracious in sharing their experience and information. Particular thanks go to the members of the Cumberland Gap Study Group, whose expertise and support have been invaluable; to Jana Lane, who typed and prepared the work and corrected my spelling; and to Gary Toms and Fran Carter, who showed me how to make a research trip. My special gratitude goes to LaVeta Capps and Margaret McCoy, who took the time to read the manuscript and make numerous vital suggestions, and to Beverly Whitaker, whose ideas, editorial advice, and wealth of knowledge made the book possible—her encouragement was no small part of the endeavor.

# INTRODUCTION

A systematic approach is critical to the success of any research trip. Without a rational, organized plan you will miss vital data, waste time, and overlook clues that you will not discover until you have returned home. When taking even a brief trip, a step-by-step approach—from the initial planning, through the trip itself, to the follow-up work when you return—will give you unexpected rewards in your research progress.

Many colleges teach students to expect to spend two hours of study for each hour of class. Apply this principle to your trip planning—two hours of preparation for each hour you expect to spend in a research facility or historic area. This means *advance* work—not the evaluation you will be doing during the trip. The extra hours will require dedication but will be time well spent.

The success of your trip depends on the preparation of your materials, your procedures, and yourself:

- Your files and equipment will have given you a foundation to work smoothly and efficiently.

- Your knowledge of the basic techniques, and your skill in dealing with people and institutions, will have brought you a variety of information.

- Your attitude of friendliness and openness to new experiences, combined with a professional and systematic approach, will have made your research thorough and comprehensive.

You can return home with a sense of accomplishment that you left well prepared, did your best, and will now use your research to bring your family a deeper understanding of their heritage.

## CHAPTER 1

# What You Do at Home Saves Time on the Road

*It was a beautiful autumn day when we started on our first—and only—genealogical research trip. We had really planned to visit my sister in Florida, but when the nieces and nephews came down with chicken pox, and we had to change our plans, Bob suggested we head for Kentucky and check out his family history. I protested at first. I'd been with him to the library a few times and wanted no part in all that microfilm reading and those books with fine print.*

*"But this will be just like a vacation, Bev," he told me.*

*So I agreed, reluctantly.*

*"Won't we need to do some things first?"*

*"No," he said as he tossed several boxes of papers in the trunk. "I have all my files here, and we're packed for Florida anyway."*

*So off we went, determined to find his ancestral home and fill in all the blank spaces on his pedigree charts . . .*

## Selection of the Area

The selection of your research site may be determined by circumstances you cannot control completely. If you need to be in a particular location because of business or other needs, it makes sense to do genealogical work in that area also. Even a few hours in a library or record center can be helpful. If, however, you are deciding about your trip on a genealogical basis primarily, then you have a choice of approaches to your selection of the area.

There can be a special satisfaction in following your ancestors backward in their actual migration pattern, moving from one place to another as they did. It will give you a sense of their life you cannot get otherwise. Start by making a migration map, using the data you have accumulated already. Begin your trip at the most recent known residence; do your research there and move on to the place your ancestors lived before that. When you are satisfied you have looked thoroughly in one area, go on to the next. This backwards approach allows you to get the feel of the migration and still change search areas, if you discover that someone did not come from the area from which you thought he had come. A trip like this takes time, of course. However, if necessary, the trip can be done in segments, visiting a few spots and traveling a short distance on each trip you make.

A more concentrated approach, and one that is especially effective if you have several family lines in one area, is to concentrate on that area and exhaust the possible records for all the surnames you are researching there. This gives you maximum opportunity to discover unusual sources and to make full use of library and archival material.

There may be times when you will not be searching particular lines as much as investigating research centers themselves. A trip to the LDS Family History Library in Salt Lake City, Utah, or to several libraries and archives in a geographic area may give you information on many ancestors and requires special preparations for visiting the facilities as well.

Whichever approach you choose, know that it is important to keep your expectations reasonable. If you do not, you are certain to be disappointed. You cannot believe you will find *everything* in one trip. Relax and enjoy what you do find. Good preparation will be the major factor in success, but, even with the best preparation, much research is not going to result in major discoveries.

Remember to take other factors into consideration in planning your trip. Weather can certainly affect your decisions, especially when traveling by car. County roads can become inaccessible in winter, and rain and snow can limit visits to cemeteries or family farms. High humidity and heat can cause discomfort, particularly in some county courthouses without adequate air-conditioning in storage areas. In a large city, transportation may be affected by the weather, and even walking a few blocks can be uncomfortable, especially if you are carrying genealogical material.

Be sure also to take into account the availability of recreational opportunities when deciding on the area you will visit.

It can be very satisfying to mix research with sightseeing at historic and scenic spots. Such activity not only gives you an understanding of the land but a needed break from intense study. A special event or place—historical pageant, fair, hobby workshop, amusement park, etc.—can give an added dimension to the trip.

## Study of Local History and Geography

If you can see the geography and history of your ancestors' land as the setting for the family migration pattern, you will have made great progress in understanding your genealogy. It is essential that you see your people in the context of their place in time and in the land. They did not just *visit* in places like Virginia.

They *lived* there and were affected by the weather and politics; when they moved on to a specific place, there was a reason for their selection. Use what you have as clues as to where you should search on your trip. (For example, if you know your ancestors were in the vicinity of the 1811–12 New Madrid earthquake, then plan to search land records, since land in the public domain was used to replace holdings damaged by the quake. Much of the property was sold to speculators, and some claims lasted for years.) There is a quantity of material available that can point to your family's presence in particular places.

As you study, coordinate past and present geography. The rivers will probably (but not always) stay the same; highways will replace trails and county roads; towns will appear and disappear; so work with both new maps and those for the period you are researching. The county highway departments are good sources for up-to-date maps, and historical atlases and local historical societies can supply the older ones. Be especially aware of places no longer in existence. These can be found in various area source-books. Both place names and names of stores and companies are clues to surnames, also, so look at old business directories if they are available to you.

It is essential that you know your political history. Always be aware that records may be kept by the parent county, not the most recently formed one. Do not make a long trip to the wrong place. Determine as best you can in advance what records were taken by that county. Examine other political entities—towns, special tax districts, etc.—so you are thoroughly familiar with what will be available locally. Determine which of the records can be searched through your home resources, and do this as part of your advance work. (A special point: do not leave home without having checked *every* census record for the possible residence of your people. If you do this you will know exactly where to search, and, since census records are readily available, you will not waste travel time finding information you could have located at home or visiting courthouses that have no information for you.)

Spend time studying the history of the area. Know what wars might have affected it. For example, imagine the movement of southern sympathizers in Missouri during years of border warfare or the Loyalist families who fled to Canada during the American Revolution. Learn what religious groups settled the land, what languages and ethnic populations were represented, and what prominent people affected the community. Did Daniel Boone lead your people west? Did your Quaker ancestors experience persecution? Was cheaper land available or bounty land given? Did any oldest son give up his inherited land because of worn-out soil or drought? Did a younger son without land seek his fortune elsewhere, excited by some discovery of gold or new territory? Each aspect of land history is a clue to family history. The land, its history, and your family are inseparable.

Do not neglect the obvious when you are studying. Send for tourist information. It is usually filled with a wealth of background detail. It will not only guide you to vacation experiences on your trip but may give you valuable research information. Travel clubs and local chambers of commerce are good sources and offer detailed local maps.

## Advance Work:
## Records, Knowledge, and Contacts

Know what you have and what you need to look for. Once more, we need to say: do not waste time on a trip getting information in person that you could obtain by correspondence or phone. Save your travel time for what you can get only in the area itself. Censuses, wills and estate records, deaths, marriages, and deeds usually can be obtained without leaving home. Write for as much as you can before you leave. Such advance work has three advantages: It saves you time and effort in your on site research; it can lead you to original material (for example, an index to wills searched in your local library can help you find an original will a clerk has been unable to send you); and it can give you clues to other data you did not know existed. An example of this might be a reference to a marriage that leads you to some small local church and its pastor's personal wedding records.

Organize and analyze your own files first, then look for clues. Be aware of missing data and inconsistencies or unusual situations. There are usually three or four generations in each century (occasionally two or five). More or less can point to a possible error in the material. A difference of more than ten years in age between husband and wife can indicate a second marriage. Being familiar with your own records is essential to adding to your knowledge and filling up those blank spaces on your charts. This study will help you know what to look for and prepare you to change your mind about any suspicious entries.

Use family traditions as clues to plan your trip. There is almost always some grain of truth in these stories. They often get attached to the wrong generation or to a sibling or cousin, but there is usually some basis for reality. A "war hero" and "officer" may really have been only a six-month enlisted private, but his military records will be just as valuable to you as if he had been a general. Think about each tradition to see what it *could* mean.

Never neglect to include allied family names in your research. The man your great-great *aunt* married may have left valuable information about your *mother* because his biography may include his wife's family, which, of course, is yours also. This is a way of getting help you might never get otherwise.

While you are examining your records, prepare yourself for your trip by becoming as skilled as you can in the knowledge you need to be an efficient genealogist. Start by learning the law in the area of your research. Laws and records vary greatly. If you are familiar with the way a death or land transaction is handled, you will not miss documents that are unique to a particular county or state; some papers are held by a division of the system that would not be expected to have such records. Learn legal terms also, including obsolete ones. This is essential in understanding the papers you find.

Learn about date changes— not just the Julian-Gregorian change, but the Quaker church calendar also. Be aware of the European way of stating dates, with the numbers representing the month and day, the reverse of our system.

Study early handwriting forms. There are excellent books to help you deal with this often-neglected skill.

Spend time learning about library research techniques. The Dewey Decimal System and card catalogs are just the beginning. Learn to cope with genealogical filing systems and with new computerized ways to access library material. Practice your library skills at home before you leave on your trip.

Talk with others who have been to the region. You will be surprised by the help they can give you. Look for members of local genealogical organizations who can tell you of their travel experiences and offer details on getting the most out of your trip. These people can be a very valuable source of information.

While you are doing your self-preparation, start reaching out to the area in which you will travel. By collecting information and establishing personal contacts you are laying a foundation for your actual work there.

Start by asking the libraries and research centers you will be visiting to send you a description of their holdings. You might even consider using a form for this purpose so the librarian or archivist can enter the information you need in an organized way. State the geographical region and the time period in which you are interested and ask for any specific records you think they might have. Then ask for "other data" in your area of interest and for "other sources" they suggest you search. Leave space for a statement of hours and holiday closings and for their copying policy and costs. Be sure to ask for any handouts and enclose an SASE large enough to hold them. A very short note with the form will express your thanks in advance for their cooperation.

Use source-books found in genealogical libraries to locate family surname organizations. Write and ask them for membership rosters, copies of newsletters, and information regarding private libraries. By making personal contact you may discover others working on the same lines as you. If no formal organization exists, the question, "Do you know anyone else working on this line?" is always a good one to ask other people.

Check the phone directory (usually for large cities these are available in public libraries) for people with your surnames. Watch for spelling variations. (A good clue is the number of syllables; the letters may vary but the number of syllables often stays constant.) For small towns, you may have to wait until you are there to check this source, but if you can do it in advance, valuable time can be saved.

Subscribing to a local newspaper for awhile can have unexpected benefits. You will learn something about current events, businesses, funeral homes, churches, organizations, and maybe find the names of local historians and feature writers. Try writing a letter to the editor of a small paper stating your genealogical interest and asking for information on his newspaper files. Some editors will not only reply but print your letter as well so you may get local response. An alternative is to advertise in the personals for information on your family. Be sure to name all siblings and allied surnames. Keep in mind that any appeal for locating people will be interpreted as a search for missing heirs, so be very clear in your statements and expect some strange replies.

Make personal contacts with everyone you possibly can. The following chapters have suggestions for establishing relationships with such people as historical society members and county clerks, but do not overlook a very special source, the local professional genealogical researcher. Try hiring someone to do a bit of work for you in advance of your arrival. If it is satisfactory try a bit more and then arrange to meet the person when you arrive. Taking a "guide" to the local research facilities will have two advantages: you will have someone who will show you exactly where to go and what to look for with no wasted time, and you will gain instant credibility with clerks and librarians. The investment of a fee for a few hours will be well spent.

In your correspondence, be brief and professional as well as friendly. Use business-like stationery and type your requests if at all possible. Letters with difficult-to-read handwriting usually remain unanswered. Do not *ever* forget the SASE. If you telephone, keep to reasonable hours and always ask if the call is convenient for the other person. Follow any call with a note expressing your gratitude for cooperation. Be quick to send the fee for any copying that is done without prior payment, and include any extra costs for postage.

Start your inquiries early. This will give you time to send a polite reminder letter if you do not receive the information in reasonable time. Write and ask if perhaps your request was not received and enclose a copy of it and another SASE. The chances are that it is stuck on a desk somewhere, but the follow-up letter will probably elicit a prompt reply. By starting your correspondence early you will also allow time to make further requests that will add to your research data and plans, and this will give you an opportunity to establish a sense of familiarity with the people you will be seeing on your trip.

Keep a copy and/or a log of all correspondence and a record of your phone calls. You need to know what you have requested, of whom and when, and you should note their reply.

If this sounds like too much work for a single trip, keep in mind that the time you spend on that trip can be doubled in productivity if you are properly prepared. Start planning early. The information and skills you acquire will benefit your research for years to come.

## CHAPTER 2

# *Practical Preparation*

*Bob really doesn't understand why I am so unhappy. We didn't take time to stop at any of the cute little craft places today. He didn't want to "waste time" shopping when there was so much to do. If we had better maps it would be easier, of course. That unpaved road we were on in the rain yesterday was rough on my nerves, and it was difficult to decide just where to go since Bob couldn't locate some of his charts when he tried to sort his papers in the motel last night. He said he wished he could remember if it was Mercer or Madison County he needed to visit first . . .*

## What to Check
## before You Leave Your House

There are basic considerations that are too often overlooked when planning a research trip. Sometimes it is the most simple thing that can spoil the whole enterprise. We have already emphasized the need for checking on the closing hours of county courthouses and libraries. Be sure you ask, either by phone or mail, about current hours for any courthouse, library, genealogical or historical society, or research center you plan to visit. Do not rely on printed information no matter how recently it was compiled. Changes can occur that can disrupt all your plans. Ask about days off, holidays, and regional events that can affect openings. (For example, Robert E. Lee's birthday—19 January —is a holiday observed in most of the southern states.) If there is a regional festival of some kind, consider it in your plans if you want to enjoy it as a vacation, but keep in mind that most local history buffs—the people you would like to talk with—will probably be too involved just before and during the celebration to have time to visit with you. Enjoy the event but stay *afterwards* to research.

Each place you search will have its own rules and regulations. Know the rules beforehand. Do not be caught with a spiral notebook when you can take only loose papers into the facility. Are "pencils only" the rule? Is identification required? Some keepers of original manuscript collections demand a photo I.D.

Be sure to ask if reservations are necessary for research. Are they good for all day or is there a time limit? Do you lose your microfilm reader if you take a lunch break? It is better to know in advance so you can have a large breakfast!

Just before you go, call the local highway department to check on road conditions. Ask about recent construction and closed or limited-access roads. One researcher we know was blocked from reaching a cemetery by a cave-in above an old rock quarry. The road was then considered too dangerous to travel. In this situation there was no alternative route, but a talk with a local authority may help you adjust your travel plans.

## What to Prepare before You Go

It is essential before you start traveling that you organize your genealogical material in such a way that you can correlate what you find and add it to your previous work. For this purpose an on-the-road filing system must be both portable and efficient.

Notebooks are heavy and usually contain more material than you need. Therefore, carrying your file notebooks (or complete file folders) would be impractical because of weight and bulk. It would also be impractical because of the chance of losing material during the trip. Since you should *always* take only duplicates of your papers, carrying complete files would necessitate much unnecessary copying of material. What you need is a system that allows you to take what is critical to your research for a particular trip and leave behind what is not essential. If you have done the preliminary work outlined in chapter 1, this should not be too difficult since you will have defined your needs rather distinctly.

A system that allows for carrying a variety of information and yet is easy to work with could be based on the pocket folders found in any office supply store. These hold 8½-by-11-inch papers in two pockets with a central section held by brads or clips. This gives you a "bound" portion and two loose paper sections. Use a different color folder for each family group or individual so that you can identify folders without looking at the labels. In the center clip section place the following:

- Pedigree charts.

- Family group sheets.

- A census record summary—one or more sheets listing the census information you have found, county by county, going back from recent to earlier times.

- A migration chart listing your ancestors in reverse chronological order as they appear in records—giving the state, county, date, and what event occurred (e.g., birth, marriage, death).

■ Your own summary of research, noting what facts you have, your conclusions, and what you plan to check on next.

■ Any other chart you find helpful.

In the pockets place the following:

■ A research check list—possible sources to remind yourself of what you have or have not investigated.

■ Research calendars on which you have recorded your work in the past so you will not duplicate effort by reexamining the same material.

■ Any miscellaneous papers you may need (for example, family group sheets for other families of the same surname may help, by elimination, to identify your particular line).

In addition to your family folders, carry one or more general folders, depending on your research plans. Contents could include the following:

■ A list—by county—of all surnames you are researching, including allied lines.

■ County information such as maps (current and historical), date of organization and parent county, and what vital records are available.

■ Information on libraries and research facilities.

■ Correspondence with local officials and researchers.

When you are designing your filing system keep in mind that you will be adding data as you travel.

Provide for placing in the family or individual folders:

- New research calendars.

- Updated conclusion/summaries.

- Updated list of things to check on.

A small amount of copied information may be added to the family folders, but also carry with you some 9-by-12-inch envelopes to hold any quantity of material you find on the trip. Label these as you use them, by surname, family, or county, so they will be in order when you get home.

Take with you whatever forms you normally use in your work. Research calendars are essential, and abstract forms will reduce greatly your time in gathering data. Various "how-to" books have examples of forms for extracting data from land records, wills, cemetery research, and more. Take a number of these forms with you and put only the ones you need into a folder each day according to what you are searching at that time.

Since you will be away from home your folders will act as your file. Have some sort of "drawer" for them. A canvas tote bag or its equivalent is generally good. You can carry it easily and set it on the floor in a library. Have some other container to leave in the car or motel room so you carry only what you need each day. Add or subtract folders as you travel. Do not keep carrying the county information from one state when you move to another or family group folders when you are in a region where that family did not live. These bags can also hold the various items you will need in research facilities.

Two final points on your portable files. *Never* carry your only copy of any material. Always make duplicates for the trip. Papers can get lost, and your copies remaining at home will keep you from having to repeat work in the future. *Always* mark everything with name, address, and phone number, including area code. Papers accidently left behind will usually be returned if they can be identified. Be prepared to mark new material you find also.

## What to Take with You

Besides your portable filing system there are many items you will find useful on the road. Some have been mentioned already and others will appear in later chapters but a summary will help you plan for your needs.

Take good clear maps. Both new and historical ones are important.

Travel/vacation guides are always useful. Keep them organized as you do your research files.

Carry any membership cards you have for genealogical and historical societies. They can gain you admittance to places you might otherwise have trouble entering. Include photo I.D. as well. Take pens, pencils, a pencil sharpener, paper clips, rubber bands (useful for rolled-up large papers), a magnifying glass, a name stamp or embosser, and envelopes to hold small items.

A pad of small notepapers can be useful for service as bookmarks and call slips. (While the peel-off kind are fine for work at home, be careful taking them to a library—librarians may be concerned about their use on valuable books.)

Have SASE's to leave where necessary.

Consider using a small easel with a magnetic board to hold papers upright in a library. These are available at office supply stores and make reading a little easier.

Consider also taking a clip board to rest on the edge of a table or to prop up on a book to change your writing angle. A cardboard insert will act as a divider for paper as you work. Anything you can do to make reading and writing more comfortable will pay off in better research.

Use pill bottles, one each for quarters, dimes, and nickels, to hold cash for photocopying. It would be very frustrating to leave behind records because the research facility had no change available. The pill bottle arrangement allows you to find the coins you need easily.

Tape recorders can be useful both for interviews and, in some cases, to "talk" yourself through material you are not allowed to copy. Do not forget fresh batteries and cassettes.

A lap-top computer might be useful in libraries.

A camera is good for recording family members, homes, cemeteries, and other items. It can also be used to copy records when photocopies are not possible. Practice at home first so you are sure of getting what you want. Film and batteries are sometimes difficult to get in small towns so take a quantity with you.

If you wear glasses or contact lenses, take an extra pair or the prescription. Think what it would mean to have broken glasses or a lost contact lens on your research trip. Eye drops, if you use them, are a real help in keeping you fresh for working. (Be sure you have had a recent eye exam.)

Do not forget any medication you usually take, and do not count on getting refills for a prescription or even favorite over-the-counter brands in out-of-the-way places. Carry what you need with you. Be aware of the increased chance for back and muscle aches and headaches as a result of sitting and reading. (You have heard of tennis elbow and writer's cramp, but when you spend half-a-day at the microfilm reader you are going to suffer from bi-focal-blur and reader-wrist!)

Women might consider taking small purses tucked in their file bags rather than separate bulky handbags. Especially in large metropolitan libraries, theft can be a problem, and a researcher concentrating on papers can be an easy target for anyone who enters the room. Librarians in some centers are careful to warn patrons of this danger, but it is a good idea to protect yourself anyway. Do not leave your purse at the table while you search shelves or the card file. Keep it with you at all times. A small purse can be carried around more easily, or one with basic items might fit in a pocket. This plan also enables you to take things more easily to lunch or on breaks. If you feel it is unsafe to leave your materials behind, at least you will not be carrying both a case and a purse.

In a restricted facility where you cannot take a purse at all, women may want to wear something with pockets to hold the locker key, a favorite pencil, and coins.

It is usually not a good idea to take books with you. You probably will not have time to read them, and you will be adding to your baggage and taking a chance on losing expensive volumes. There are, however, at least two exceptions to this. State research guides can be used as you go along—assuming you have become familiar with them before leaving home. Glossaries can be of real help in deciphering records when understanding of information is necessary before you can proceed further.

Take copies of the family photos you think will be helpful in contacts with other people.

Have a compact, complete set of tools for cemetery searches.

An obvious but essential warning. If you are traveling by public transportation, never put your research material in checked-in baggage. Carry it with you somehow, or you could find yourself at your destination with no way to start your study.

## CHAPTER 3

# On the Road

*I am very unhappy. Bob seems determined to fill every moment with research of some kind, and he keeps handing me papers and telling me to keep them in order. Last night he made me copy three pages of his notes because he said the ones he'd taken in the county museum were illegible, and he wanted his files to be neat. What does he mean by neat? I've seen some of his files, and those scraps of paper with notes in the margins couldn't be called very professional. If only I could take a walk, get some exercise, and clear my head . . .*

## Motels, Meals, and Other Necessities

The mechanics of your trip should not be allowed to overshadow its purpose, but neither should they interfere with it. Too much concentration on finding exceptional restaurants and places to stay can take away emphasis on research, but too little attention to this part of the trip can make life miserable for you.

Start your planning by realizing you often will have little choice of accommodations. Your selection will be dictated by your location, but a few suggestions may be of help.

Phone ahead your reservations to ease your travel. Since you will need to stay in specific spots, this may help you avoid a common vacationer's problem — having to drive many extra miles to find lodging and then doubling back the next day. Even if you cannot make long-range plans, at least try to call by early afternoon to reserve a place for the evening. This arrangement allows you to see how things are going in one town before you decide to move on. Choose your motel location based on your research needs and your own pattern of living. If you are an early riser, you may prefer to spend the night in the town you have been working in and drive on in the morning before the courthouse opens in the next county; if you are a night owl then drive on in the evening and get up just before the courthouse opens in the next town. Do whatever is comfortable. You will feel better, and your research will improve when you are rested and alert.

Remember to take anything you need for special problems or comfort. A neck pillow for the car, a special pillow for the motel, or anything that makes you feel better is worth taking.

Coordinate your meals with your research. Just because you always eat at a certain time at home does not mean you cannot adapt to a new situation. Eat when research centers are closed, if possible, and when it is too dark to search cemeteries.

Take, or buy, healthy snacks for remote locations or awkward times where you cannot get a regular meal.

Try buying deli-type food for an impromptu picnic on a day you plan to search a cemetery. If you have space, put a small ice chest in your car so picnic arrangements will be easier to make. Always carry a knife and can opener with you for unexpected treats. Fresh fruits often can be purchased in country locations and make a nice addition to routine diets.

Allot adequate time for meals and rest. Do not rush eating or constantly short yourself on sleep. You will function more smoothly if you follow good health practices.

Be sure to allow time for relaxation exclusive of sleep and meals. Do not rush madly from one research problem to another. Take time to unwind and also to get some exercise. You will need it if you are sitting each day indoors. Walk around in the library itself, at least every hour or so. Stretch a bit when you can. Walk around your motel or the town, if possible.

Walking can do much more than give you exercise. It can be a key to helping you "feel" the area. Really *look* at the land your ancestors lived on — see the hills, the trees, the old buildings. If they still exist, find houses, schools, churches, and businesses your ancestors once lived in or visited. Imagine your ancestor playing in a park or fishing in a stream. Using your imagination is as essential as using your intellect in understanding your history. One genealogist found a strong sense of family by visiting the cabin her great-great-great-great grandfather built. It still exists in a restored historic park in her native town. The tool marks on the logs give her a real feeling of connection with the past. She says it made her family group sheet come alive to imagine the house being built and the family being inside those walls. Combine activities like this with rest and relaxation, and you will have added to your research in many ways.

## Maintaining a Systematic Research Approach

The foresight and effort you have given to your trip planning will pay dividends on the road if you maintain a systematic approach to your research.

Discipline yourself to enter any data you discover in the proper place in your research system. Do not scribble unintelligible notes on scraps of paper. Use those forms you started on and stick to the system. Whatever data entry forms (research calendars, abstract sheets, etc.) you use, make sure material is entered clearly and completely.

Avoid writing so fast you will be forced to recopy data later. The more copying, the more mistakes are possible. Try to make the first copy the final one.

Be sure to note on the paper itself, where and when you found each item. (And, once more, do not forget to stamp your name, address, and phone number on each paper.)

Add names and information to your work sheet, pedigree chart, and family group sheet in a different color ink so you can evaluate your findings later and know what to add to your permanent charts at home.

During the day, find time for a brief review and evaluation of what you are doing. Extend your lunch break for an extra ten minutes, and decide if you are on the right track or need to change direction for the afternoon work.

Earlier, we stated the benefits that could result from spending two hours in preparation for every one hour you expect to spend in a research facility. Now apply that same idea to your research during the trip itself. Find time each evening (or sooner, if practical) to read over what you have found while it is still fresh in your mind. Look at it and see how it fits in with what you already have. Watch for clues. Think about what the information means. Any material deserves another hour of study done in a better setting and when you are more relaxed. You may be surprised by what you will discover in that second reading.

Keep up daily with your system of noting what you have done and plan to do. Use your research item checklist and write new summaries or speculations. This takes very little time and effort and will be of immense use in clarifying your thinking.

## CHAPTER 4

# Getting to Know Your Relatives

*It was a real shock to meet Cousin Jane. When Bob first wrote to her years ago to get some information, she had seemed friendly enough. Maybe it was the way we phoned and said we were coming by in twenty minutes to see her that made her a little cranky. It probably was a bad time to visit since she was in the middle of apple butter season, but we explained we had to hurry so we could get on to the next town. We'd missed it once already because we had to circle around the county since the road had been changed after our map was printed, and the new construction held us up. Jane said she understood, but she was downright uncooperative—wouldn't even come out of the kitchen to pose for a picture . . .*

## Strategy
## for Successful Visits

Idcally, you will have been in contact with long-distance relatives before you plan a visit with them. Every effort should have been made to establish a friendly relationship that promises to benefit them as well as you. The best initial approach is to get in touch by mail or phone and say you are sending information you have on the family. When you send this, include two copies each of pedigree charts and family group sheets. The relatives can keep one copy and add to, or correct, the other and return it to you. This is a good basis for starting a dialogue on the family history and enables you all to see where you agree or disagree on family information. Few people can resist reading these forms and "correcting" your "misconceptions."

If contact has been made only recently with these people, then prepare to send such information immediately even if you must mail it just in advance of leaving home. At least this gives them something to think about before you meet them.

When arranging the actual visit, state clearly what your plans are, especially if your relatives have invited you to stay with them. Your time of arrival and departure will affect their schedules, so be both considerate ("When will it be convenient for you?") and specific ("I will take the old highway from the north and arrive about seven o'clock. Don't bother about dinner; I'll get a bite to eat on the way down.") Indicate where you plan to stay if you are not staying with them, and offer to take them to dinner the first day. This is a good ice-breaker for strangers whose relationship has been established only by charts, not by acquaintance. If your plans change, always phone so they can make any adjustments in their activities. If you are staying with people in their homes, be especially careful of intruding. Check on bedtime and bath hours, meals, smoking policy, and other details of daily living. Carry a telephone credit card so you will not need to run up charges on their phone.

In any contact—initial or as a prelude to your first visit—state your intentions. They may be wondering what you want. Are you trying to claim land or heirlooms, dispute a will, or borrow money? Explain your interest in family history and why meeting them is important to you.

Do not be easily discouraged. One researcher was bewildered by a woman who was totally uncooperative in discussing her husband's lineage. The wife evaded talk of any meeting with him and made it impossible for the genealogist to continue contact. Only when the couple filed for divorce was it apparent the wife was not hostile but simply disinterested in her soon-to-be ex-husband's family. Later the researcher was able to meet him and a good exchange of information resulted. Do not always assume that apparent disinterest is related to you or your research. There may be other factors involved that you know nothing about. Be patient, and try again later. When relatives show a reluctance to talk with you, they may be wary of revealing family skeletons. Your assurance that you will exercise discretion is important. Stress that you want to know the truth for "historical" reasons but that you have no plans to publish it. They may not accept your offer to be discreet, but you have little recourse if they are the only source of certain material. You may have to spend years gaining their trust. You could try showing them some of your files and making reference to other genealogists who are careful in what they reveal. But your own professional manner will be your greatest asset.

If you encounter cooperative relatives then you are fortunate. Ask if you can tape interviews with them. Be prepared with questions that stimulate full answers, not just yes-and-no replies. Always ask them for "additional information" they might want to give. Make it clear you are interested in all aspects of your family's history.

Take copies of family photographs with you. Share them with the relatives. They may recognize the people or date the photos by buildings or setting. One researcher was able to better trace her family when a relative recognized the building behind Great-Grandpa as the train depot in a distant county. The researcher had never looked there for family records. Photos of buildings can also establish dates for people. Local history enthusiasts can tell you when a clock was added to a tower or a trolley line was started.

Give your relatives copies of the photos that are of special interest to them. You can have the copies made in advance if you are certain of their interest, have them made while you are in the area, or offer to send them when you get back home.

Ask to see your relative's photos. You should be familiar with books that offer help in photo identification (see the Bibliography). Look for dates, studio names or stamps on the back of photos, clothing styles to establish periods of dress, and even the order of placement in old albums. (For example, husbands' and wives' likenesses may have been placed opposite each other.) If your relatives are cooperative, try to arrange for copies to be made for you. They may feel uncomfortable letting you borrow the pictures for copying but might accompany you to a local studio for on-the-spot work. As a last resort, take your own photos of the family pictures.

Whatever pictures you do exchange, always identify them with names of people, places, and dates, noting you or your relatives as the source of the photos and the date on which the prints were given to each other.

Do not forget to take photos or video recordings of your relatives!

An important point for your relationship with these people is to be tactful when there is a disagreement over genealogical data. If someone insists your information is wrong, do not argue. Simply write down what he tells you. (After all, he could be right!) Conflicting material should be noted in your records, evaluated, and saved until the facts can be determined positively. Keep in mind the point about there being some truth in most family traditions. Above all, end your visit on a harmonious level, laying a foundation for future exchanges.

If you like, it is a nice gesture to leave a small gift for your host. One thoughtful genealogist made a lasting impression on newly found relatives by cross-stitching a music box lid with the family surnames. Those people will never forget her or her genealogical searches.

When you return home send a note of thanks for the hospitality you received, especially mentioning the genealogical help they gave you. Reinforce your relatives' sense of cooperation by sending them copies of any information you found on your trip.

## Unusual Ways to Contact Unknown Relatives

Suppose that you are in the unpleasant position of not having any relatives to visit in the area of your trip. You feel certain that there must be cousins still living in the region, but how do you discover them?

Start with the most simple approach—ask the relatives you *do* know if they have ever met, or heard of, cousins back in the home territory. Your second cousin just may tell you she has been corresponding with Grandma So-and-So for fifty years. Do not neglect to ask the same question of friends of the family. After all they may have relatives that know your relatives. Keep following the chains of both kinship and acquaintance. (Be careful not to overlook variations of your surname. Distance and time can bring about strange occurrences in spelling.)

Next, check phone directories for your surname, as suggested in chapter 1. This is quite productive at times.

Once you are in touch with family-name societies, older people in the community you are searching, and historical and genealogical societies, ask if there have been any reunions for your family names. If there have been, ask who would have the guest list and if there was any publicity you could read. People who come to reunions usually want to share information.

Write to the newspaper editor (see chapter 1) or run an ad in the personals column of the local paper (for example, "Anyone related to, or who knows the family of . . ."). You may get some local press coverage, and your ad will get attention since, even if your relative does not see it, someone will probably tell him about it. Be sure to include siblings and allied lines.

Try asking if you can put a note on the bulletin board of the local library, asking to contact relatives. Print the surnames in large letters to catch the eye of passers-by.

Do the same thing on supermarket bulletin boards. In a small town there may be only one large store so this is a good place to get everyone's attention.

Write to, or visit, local retirement and nursing homes to see if they will place your notice in their newsletter. Most will be cooperative if you explain your purpose.

Write to, or visit, churches and fraternal organizations with the same notice. Choose those that seem to fit your family's background.

Local politicians can often be of help. They are usually anxious to please, especially if they think you might have cousins of voting age. Just say things like, "I know my family and their friends will appreciate you helping me . . ." This works especially well in election years, of course. Remember politicians can check voter lists and all the other sources they use for their own campaigns.

A strange but effective method can work wonders. Someone visited an old cemetery and discovered her ancestor's grave had fresh flowers placed on it. She was at a loss to explain this since she knew of no relatives in the area. The cemetery was not connected with an organization or church, and she could locate no sexton or caretaker. Anxious to contact the donor of the flowers she put a note, with her name, address, and phone number, into a plastic sandwich bag and taped it to the tombstone. Within a month she had found a cousin she had never known existed.

Remember the warning. Any request for missing relatives will bring you odd replies. Many will come forward trying to claim the inheritance they think you are going to offer, and others will wonder about your motives and whether you have an honest reason to look for them. Be patient, explain yourself clearly, and hope for the best.

## CHAPTER 5

# Visits to Libraries and Archives

*Today was really a waste. Bob found the library all right, but we couldn't park the car in the lot so I had to keep going out every thirty minutes to put money in the meter. Then Bob said he couldn't find anything. It wasn't like using our own library. He just couldn't make sense of the books and files, and the librarian wouldn't help. She kept telling him to use the Dewey Decimal System. He told me he didn't know those numbers on the books at home were that impor- tant, and anyway these weren't the same books. He finally did find one that told about his great-grandmother's people but he was pretty sure they had that one in the library back home . . .*

## Planning
## Your Approach

Earlier we referred to the need to know what research centers are in your travel area and the impor- tance of becoming familiar with them before leaving home. This should not be too difficult. The directory published by the American Library Association will guide you to those resources, and a variety of genealogical reference and how-to books will list archives and local collections. Be alert for small, specialized libraries that may have unusual material not found elsewhere.

Always follow the basic procedure of talking with others who have been to the facility: write for information (as suggested in detail in chapter 1) and read about the content of the collection and how it is cataloged. Approach a strange library as you would a new town. For the town, you would get a map; know where the shopping centers, motels, and restaurants are; and find out how the streets are identified so you can reach your destination. Apply this procedure to the library. Be as familiar with it as you can *before* you arrive.

Once you are in the facility, allow time to get acquainted with it. Do not expect, no matter how complete your preparation, to start researching immediately. Take time to become oriented. Locate the areas of material that interest you most. Check the catalog system and ask the librarian or archivist to help you if you are not at ease with it. Do some browsing in open stacks to locate books you did not realize were available. Even thirty minutes spent before you start researching will save you a great deal of disorganization during the rest of your visit and may prevent you from overlooking important books or papers. This get-acquainted time is especially critical if you have not had the opportunity to prepare well for your visit.

If you are planning to spend some time in a particular facility, consider investing a small amount of money in hiring a local genealogist to accompany you. Such a person could show you in a short time what you need to search and get you started on your work. You could find that you have saved yourself many otherwise wasted hours by getting this expert guidance.

While you are using any particular center do not forget to ask if there are other collections in the area. The professionals will almost always know of any other specialized resources not noted in the reference books. They may have a list of these available for patrons.

If you act professionally you will be more likely to get full cooperation from the library staff. A researcher who appears to be well prepared and efficient in his approach to the facility will be treated with greater courtesy and is likely to be told more than the visitor who comes in with a ragged clutch of papers and asks aimless questions. A good example of this advantage of professionalism was given by a woman who entered an archives one morning knowing she had only that day to accomplish her research goals in the area. When the archivist saw her paper preparation and her well-defined questions, he gave her a half-hour personal tour of the center, which enabled her to work effectively the rest of the time.

## Making the Most of Your Research Time

A few guidelines will ease your research work and bring greater productivity.

Realize that you must adapt to the schedules and rules of the library, no matter what you think of them. The rules usually reflect a real concern for the genealogical materials and for other patrons. Do not ask to stay past closing or take in a pen when it is forbidden or request too many books at one time. You will just create a tense atmosphere with the staff and decrease your chance for full cooperation.

Be sure to bring proper tools with you. Like the pencils or loose paper already mentioned, there are the essentials you do not want to be caught without when you need to be working. Review the list in chapter 2 and add your own items to it.

Concentrate on what is unique to this facility. Each library or archives has material no other probably

has. You may find the only extant copies of city directories. Look at these carefully and note the names of
the neighbors of your ancestors. Remember people
often moved together to a new location, and these other
surnames may help you find and identify your family
elsewhere. Watch for unique maps in the special collections. Some may list property holders and give exact
descriptions of the land so you can locate deeds. Check
for the newspapers of local ethnic groups. These are
just a few examples of items unlikely to be found in
more than one facility. Search the special things first
since you may not see them elsewhere.

Be sure to check any surname file, the library's
card index, or a query file belonging to the library or a
genealogical society. (Always leave your own surnames
in a query file.)

Have your search plans clearly defined *including
alternate plans.* Do not make the mistake of having
your research goals so narrow that when they are
frustrated by lack of material or a dead end of some
kind, you do not know what to do next. Take a few
minutes break and start in a new direction.

Remember that indexes and abstracts are not
always complete or always accurate. They were compiled by people who are fallible human beings and so
may have misspelled or missing entries. It is critical
that you go to the original material for two reasons:
first, if you find your ancestor's listing, the information
contained in the index or abstract may not be complete.
The original may give you details not entered into the
index or abstract. For example, a marriage list may
contain the date and the names of the bride and groom,
but the original may contain the name of the minister,
name of the church, and names of parents, and witnesses (who were often relatives). Second, if you find
nothing in the index or abstract, check the original, if
at all practical, because the indexer may have
misspelled the names or omitted the listing completely.

Do not dismiss a source until you have exhausted the original.

Even if your eyes are in perfect condition, be sure to treat them well. You want to be able to work effectively the next day so do not overdo. Experienced researchers learn to look away at intervals from a microform reader, blink frequently to avoid staring at the screen, and change pace by examining card files or looking at printed matter as a relief from searching filmed records.

Do not forget about reservations for research or for microfilm readers. Even a phone call, twenty-four hours ahead, could save you disappointment.

Try to time your visit so you do not attempt to use a library or other facility at its busiest time. Saturdays and evenings are often when rooms are crowded, and librarians are not able to give a great deal of time to each patron. Ask the librarian when it is best—and worst—to come. A local facility may present a real problem if members come there before or after a genealogical meeting in the building. The librarian will know about these and other concerns.

Keep in mind that a friendly and sympathetic librarian or archivist can be your greatest research asset.

## CHAPTER 6

# Treasures of Historical, Genealogical, and Lineage Societies

*Today might have been better if that nosy woman had let us alone. We met her when we stopped to eat a snack in the town square across from the courthouse. She was putting flowers by some sort of war memorial, and all she wanted to talk about was the war— Civil War, probably—and ask questions about what we were doing. Said she belonged to some local historical society. She seemed to be nice, but we were trying to find some names in our files and really didn't have time to talk with her . . .*

## Personal Contacts
## That Can Result in Lasting Friendships

It is easy to see that the national records of various groups arc invaluable to the genealogist. Every effort should be made to search these sources and learn if your ancestors' personal history is a part of the record's accumulated data. Even the most slender clue can lead to an abundance of genealogical and historical information, since these societies have spent decades concentrating on acquiring and preserving material you are anxious to find. What we may overlook, however, is the special opportunity a research trip presents to make use of these groups in a personal way.

Each society, no matter how large its national (or even international) membership, is made up of individuals. Some of these may simply enjoy the benefits of an association passed on to them and have little interest in research themselves. Others may take deep interest in finding out more about their family history. A trip can give you an opportunity to search out these committed individuals and employ their knowledge to advance your own research work.

It is axiomatic that those in an area will know best where local records are kept. Suppose you have a Revolutionary War ancestor who lived in a particular county. It makes sense to assume that a local DAR member will have some idea of the veteran's presence in her area. Did your ancestor fight in a Civil War battle? A local interest group will probably be able to provide you with several people who can add great detail to your family history. Are you searching for a burial site? Try the special associations founded to preserve the records of old cemeteries.

A trip enables you to go beyond inquiries and written requests for information. It gives you the opportunity to make friends with these people and to enlist them as allies in your research.

Start by making contact; use the genealogical reference sources for locating the various national societies. Write to the headquarters and ask for the name of an officer of a local chapter. Then write to that person stating your plans to travel in his or her area and outline your genealogical interest. Keep your initial letter brief and include some information, such as a pedigree chart. Ask for the name of someone who might be willing to correspond with you about your research questions. If you are lucky, you will be put in touch with a member who has a great interest in local history. Write to her and offer to share information you already have. This establishes your willingness to exchange data and makes you a partner, not just an anonymous plea for assistance.

Once you have exchanged some correspondence, enlarge your circle of research by asking your new friend to suggest other people to whom you can write. The chances are she will offer these names to you before you even request them. Follow up on each suggestion until you have a pool of interested, willing helpers ready to greet you when you arrive in their community. These are the people who will take you to the historic sights, introduce you to the librarian, and see that you do not overlook anything that will aid you in your research. (They will also save you from hiring a professional!)

You, in turn, will treat them as friends. Take them to lunch, spend time admiring and appreciating the local scenery and natural beauty and learning about your friends' own research interests. Never allow them to feel "used." Show your gratitude as you would with relatives you are visiting. Gifts and thank-you notes will let them know you appreciate their help.

If circumstances prevent you from establishing a relationship slowly (by beginning in advance of your trip), then make the best of the situation. Even if you meet someone unexpectedly in the middle of your travels, you can still lay the foundation for a relationship and reap some of the benefits even in a few hours of acquaintance. Just apply the same procedure as you would when starting by correspondence.

## Museums and Other Resources That Can Aid Research

Just as there are special individuals that can help you, so there are often surprising genealogical finds where you would not expect to locate your family history. Museums have a wide range of material, even those that seem to specialize in rather narrow interests; patrons often donate things unrelated to the original collection, and these are usually stored, not discarded or passed on somewhere else. Do not take it for granted that a museum specializing in railroad history may not have a record of frontier scouts, or a historic jail may not have the log books for a local grain mill. Ask what records are available—be specific. Ask for anything that includes *names.*

Each time you visit a museum or see a collection, ask who else has historic material. One curator will usually know another. Ask for an introduction to the next one and keep searching.

Be aware of the names of donors. If the donations are frequent and the dates are recent, ask to meet the person. A donor is often a collector, too, and probably has valuable material he has not given to a public or private museum. Once you establish yourself as a serious, responsible genealogist you may be able to search his materials for unique personal information.

It is always a good idea to ask about local publications. There is often no way to discover these except through the people in the area. Many local publications are not listed in genealogical publications or exchanged with libraries. Ask society members, museum heads, and others what is being published. There may be small newsletters or columns in newspapers that will have names, dates, and events important to you.

It is worth noting that you should not overlook memorials and monuments. The most common kind, war memorials, can contain names, dates, and military units. Others may record names of those involved in local disasters, the erection of buildings, or the dedication of parks. Ask for directions to these as you expand your local contacts.

When it is practical, join such groups as local associations and museum societies as a sign of your interest and a means of receiving information in the future. A small donation to museums is almost always appreciated.

The key is always to see the human side of history and look for the personal records your ancestors left within the community record. The individuals you meet today are the custodians of that history and your best guide to the genealogy within it.

## CHAPTER 7

# Approaching Courthouses

*I have never seen such rude people! Bob just wanted to find his great-great-grandfather's marriage license and maybe his death certificate, and that clerk wouldn't even look for them. She denied the county kept those records. Bob said he knew better. She just didn't want to go back and find them. (I did feel a little sorry for her, though. It was hot in that place even for me in my halter top and Bob in his Florida shirt and shorts.) Bob told her off good; said we're taxpayers and she ought to do what we wanted. Would you believe she said we didn't pay taxes in that county?*

## Establishing Yourself as a Researcher, Not a Nuisance

Contacts with county clerks and other officials can be frustrating. Whereas libraries and historical societies employ people to help the patron or visitor with his work, the county personnel are hired to do *county* business, not help genealogists. They are trained and get paid to keep the records, collect taxes, and assist in the settlement of legal questions. As an outsider, not even a taxpayer of that county, it is up to you to be as professional as possible and as self-reliant as you can be. There are several things you can do to give yourself the greatest chance for success in your research.

Start by writing in advance of your visit, requesting some item of information from the county records. This accomplishes two things. It establishes your identity, at least with a small county in which there is only one or maybe two clerks. Second, it gives you the name of that clerk so you now have a person, not just a title, to contact.

(Keep a record of this correspondence, of course. Know what you requested, when you requested it, and the results. Send a very polite, follow up letter if you hear nothing in a month. Include a second SASE.)

When you have received an answer to your letter, send for something else. Keep your requests simple. Remember you are trying to establish a working relationship. You want the clerk to feel a sense of partnership. Mention that you are planning a visit to the county, that you think that there is material there, that you know that it would be difficult for the clerk to take the time to locate the material, and you are anxious to conduct a search in her "fine record center."

When you arrive at the courthouse, look professional. People do react to our appearance. Dress as you would to conduct business, not have a vacation. Three piece suits and ties are not necessary, but shorts, bare feet, and sandals detract from your ability to get clerks to take you seriously. Look as if you mean business, and you will usually get a businesslike response. This is not the place for the flowered tote bag or the amusing genealogical pin. Save these for activities at home, among friends.

Have the tools of your trade with you. Do not ask to use the clerk's paper or pencils. Come prepared with whatever may be necessary to record what you find. Act professional. Start by getting to the point of your visit. Do not launch into a lengthy description of how many years you have been doing genealogy, of how important it is to you to find records of Great-Grandpa, or start telling about your family history. The clerk has her work to do, and even if she is not busy she does not really want to hear the details of your research. Remember you are still a stranger to her.

Start by making specific requests. Be alert to what books or files she brings you, where they are stored, and what else might be there. Do not ask for more than one or two things at a time.

Be friendly. Brevity in requests does not mean a demanding attitude. A smile, a polite phrasing of a sentence, and an expression of gratitude take no more time than a disagreeable expression and a rude manner.

Be aware of office procedures. Observe closing hours (and lunch hours in small counties). Remember that courthouses usually close early. Try to arrange your trip so you work there first, then move on to a library or other resource.

It is imperative that you make every effort to know exactly what records are available in the county. Genealogical reference books can help greatly. There is no point in demanding death records if these are kept only by the state. Do not insist on finding marriage records before the time the law mandated they be recorded. Go to the courthouse with the knowledge of what you can reasonably expect to find there. With this confidence you can feel secure in *gently* suggesting that the clerk may have some information you need.

Do not, however, always conclude that a county has only what is listed in the reference books. Some counties may have kept their own records separate from state listings or started recording vital statistics before they were officially supposed to do so.

Always ask for "other records." Your advance study of legal recording procedures will help, but ask the clerk such questions as the following:

- ■ "What would have happened to records of . . . ?"

- ■ "What would be the next legal step?"

- ■ "Were these things always entered in the deed books or are they found in other places?"

Remember it is not uncommon to find totally different kinds of records entered in the same book.

Try to be informed in advance of not only what records were kept but what those records contained. It does no good to spend time looking for marriage records in order to find the groom's parents' names if local marriages never listed this information. Books such as *The Source: A Guidebook of American Genealogy* (see the Bibliography) are helpful in telling you what is included in various documents.

Stay constantly aware of the significance of details in what you find. If you have done your homework properly you know that documents offer subtle clues in the material they contain. There is a pattern of evidence you should not ignore. A few illustrations will give you an idea of what to watch for:

- ■ Remember that in documents conveying land, about two thirds of the time each side of the family provided two of the witnesses. Do not overlook their names.

- ■ In marriage records, also, the witnesses were usually relatives.

- ■ Death certificates are useful even if the information is often inaccurate. Check the person giving the family history. Almost always this was a relative. A father, a woman's brother, a son-in-law, all give clues to maiden names and marriages.

- ■ Always be alert to variations of both surnames and given names. As we stated earlier the number of syllables is often an indication one name is a variation of another.

As you search for information be prepared to record it. Abstract forms are useful and practical. Carry a few with you since copies of county records may be very expensive. Always check the price of the work before you ask for copies of twenty pages of estate and probate information. You might be shocked to learn it costs two dollars or more a page. If it is worth that to you, go ahead, but do not allow yourself to be trapped into an unpleasant situation. Remember, however, that copying does eliminate transcription errors.

Do not try to violate the courthouse regulations. You will probably be forbidden to do any further research if you are caught. This is *their* territory; they make the rules. Once you have established a good working relationship, the clerk may bend a few rules for you but do not expect it.

Always leave the records as you find them. Do this for the sake of other genealogists and for the clerk. Do not rearrange loose papers or "correct" items. If you feel something is an error ask the clerk if you can leave a note in the book or folder, but do not be surprised if you are turned down. Remember her job is to preserve county material not assist genealogists. Ask if you should reshelve books or return material to the vertical file. Ask what you can do to help the clerk. This is almost certain to be an unusual statement to her. Make it clear you want to assist in any way you can in getting out and dealing with material. She may not let you help, but she probably will be impressed by your sensitivity to her work load.

When you finish your visit there is often an advantage in leaving SASE's with the clerk. If you have discovered a great deal of material but do not have time to get out each book or file, leaving an SASE will allow the clerk to find the documents and send copies to you when it is convenient for her. This saves you both time and still ensures you will get the material you will need. An SASE should always be left, even if you see no immediate need for it. Leaving it and two or three dollars will encourage the clerk to think of other things to send you. Often she will realize after you have left that some document would be of interest to you, but without the SASE she probably would not send it. It is worth the gamble to gain information you may have missed.

(A minor, but often, useful, idea is to take clothes you can change into conveniently after a courthouse visit. You may find your shirt or blouse sleeves get very dirty handling old records.)

## Techniques for Making Friends with County Clerks

One point bears repetition in almost every chapter of this guide: you are dealing with people. Clerks have feelings, job problems, families, and the stresses of life common to us all. Treat them as persons and hope for a personal response.

Start by finding something to praise. (This may be difficult in some situations, but try!) Thank the clerk for the efficient way she responded to your mail inquiry. This not only makes her feel good about her work but reminds her of who you are. Comment on how well organized the facility is, how easy it is to locate, and how pleasant it is to work in. Praise her helpful attitude, or, if appropriate, compliment her on her hairstyle or dress. Find something positive to say, something that will make her feel good about talking with you. Be sincere. If you feel cheerful and positive she may respond.

Do not let the age of the clerk deter you. Do not assume a youthful one will not understand your genealogical interest. She may be an amateur historian herself, more eager to help than an older person who has become dissatisfied with her job and anxious to retire. Give her a chance to help you.

Even taking into consideration the clerk's schedule and your desire not to waste time, there will almost always be moments for personal comments and observations. Show an interest in local activities and events. The clerk may be passionately involved with the garden club, and your comments on an upcoming tulip festival will make her much more receptive to your genealogical questions. References to community history may spark her memory of local stories.

A few inquiries about her family may work wonders in establishing communication. Glancing at pictures of her grandchildren may be just what you need to keep her searching for your records. Show her that you value her family history as well as your own. It would be wonderful if her family turned out to be early settlers and she just happens to be the current town historian.

There may be times in extended research in courthouses when it is appropriate to ask the clerk to take her break or have lunch with you. Be careful to avoid misinterpretation, but sharing a meal or a snack can be a great way to get acquainted. Remember, a clerk's position may often be a relatively lonely one. She might appreciate the attention and companionship. Try asking first if she can recommend a restaurant; then suggest you would like to treat her since she has "been so helpful." Even if your gesture is declined it will be appreciated.

If you have spent considerable time in a courthouse and expect to spend more, or if your requests have been numerous and detailed, you might want to bring a small gift to the clerk. It should not be expensive and should look spontaneous, just something you "found and thought you would like." Do not overdo the gift—a plant for her desk, an attractive tissue holder, a basket for her desk accessories—just let the gift be something to show your appreciation. (Remember, most public employees are not allowed to accept gifts officially. Be sensitive to local policy.)

There is value also in remembering that the clerk has a boss somewhere. If you can establish contact with the supervisor and gain her cooperation, your relationship with the clerk will be improved. Employees want, and need, to please employers, so if you are able to arrange any meeting with her superior, use the opportunity to enhance your position with the clerk.

A subtle but effective technique can also result in increased cooperation. County clerks are elected—or at least they are hired by elected officials. Use this to your advantage even though you are not a local taxpayer. Make references to cousins and friends in the county by name if you can. If you do not know any relatives yet, say how much your family will appreciate the clerk's effort in helping you locate them. Emphasize that you will tell the local historian, the genealogist, the librarian, and anyone else you meet how you were treated at the courthouse. The point will not be lost, especially if an election is coming soon. (A warning here, do not try to research in some courthouses immediately before an election. The clerks may be too involved in partisan politics to have time to do their regular work, let alone help visiting genealogists.)

A final note. A courthouse, like a library, is a good place to take a paid or amateur researcher or a local historian. They can help you get started with your work and establish immediate credibility with the county clerk. Be a little cautious doing this. A clumsy researcher may have irritated the clerk in the past, and you do not want to be identified with the irritation. Correspond first; if a genealogist expresses hostility towards the clerk, it would be better to go alone and establish your own relationship.

## CHAPTER 8

# Finding Help in Churches

*I thought today would be better but it wasn't. We must have stopped at fifteen churches to ask for records. No one seemed to know anything. And then we got caught in a festival of some sort—Persimmon Days or something like that—and found out most places were closed, including the church offices. You would think pastors would be more dedicated. To top it all off, we couldn't even find a place to eat lunch, the restaurants were so crowded . . .*

## The Importance of Advance Contacts

Because of their great diversity of structure, religious organizations present a special challenge for the genealogical researcher. Without careful study and detailed investigation the genealogist may miss huge segments of family and historical data, especially for the nineteenth century. (Earlier records, covering the sixteenth to eighteenth centuries, are not as helpful.) This is an area where advance work can be critical.

As with other types of research, start with correspondence whenever possible. County histories usually tell you which churches were established in a community and often give the dates, and occasionally the places, the church members left in their migration to new territory. Examine the geography of your research area closely, noting the migration patterns of the population. Was there an influx of a particular denomination from the region in which you know your family once lived? If so, then your ancestors were possibly of this denomination, traveling as a congregation. Using the phone directory or information from the local historians or genealogists you have already been in touch with, learn the names of the present churches and their pastors. Use logic in choosing which ones you will contact. Study your family pattern to determine which denominations are most likely to have been their churches. Quakers moving to a new community might not remain Quakers, but they are more likely to become Baptists than Catholics. Catholics are not likely to become Presbyterians but probably would have traveled great distances to keep in touch with members of their faith.

If you have the information already, write to the oldest churches first or write the pastor you choose to contact and ask for the name the oldest local branch of his denomination. If there are strong ethnic ties in your ancestry, ask the pastor to guide you to those congregations with large numbers of your family's background.

Be aware of the splitting apart and joining of denominations. Understand how the passage of time and historical events may have affected church membership. A good example is the Civil-War-era division that resulted in the formation of the Southern Methodist denomination, its rejoining with the northern segment, and the more recent joining of that denomination with the United Brethren. Keep in mind that churches have their own "pedigree charts." Learn to read these and you will have a better chance of finding your ancestors' records.

Churches have a wide variety of record-keeping procedures. Ask if this data is centralized. (If so, you can write to the denominational headquarters or include it in another trip.) Did local or regional administrations duplicate records? Ask before you leave home.

When you write, ask the pastor for the names of local groups that use—or did use at one time—the church facilities. These secular groups usually include many church members, so your ancestors are likely to have been in these organizations also.

Ask newspapers or libraries for file information on local churches and denominations. Especially in small towns, church activities may form a major part of the social life and are reported in length. Regular meetings, special events, and noteworthy activities always get local publicity.

Historical societies may search their books to help you determine which churches to contact. Ask particularly for local anniversary publications that give accounts of the establishment of congregations.

# Locating
# Obscure Records

Once you have done some study of church history and local religious populations and have decided which churches offer the greatest opportunities for research, you will be able to travel to the community with a greater hope of finding your ancestors' records. Follow all the suggestions previously made for contacts with librarians, historians, and county clerks. Approach the pastor with the goal of enlisting him as your ally in research. Unless he is overwhelmed by work he will probably welcome your interest and your visit.

Start by asking what records he has even if you have asked for them already in correspondence. He has

had time to think since you wrote to him and may have
recalled other records he did not mention previously.
Again, ask about records kept by the headquarters of
the denomination.

Ask for "other records." He may not even consider
some information to be what you need so suggest types
of data to him. Ask about Sunday School and church
board minutes. These give many names, are always
dated, and tell you just what your ancestor was involved in at a particular time. Are there Sunday School
class rolls? These are especially good for determining
the ages and relationship of children. Are there copies
of church bulletins or newsletters? These will give
births, christenings, marriages, deaths, and reports on
the activities of members.

Transfer and membership records are especially
important since these list the place the member came
from and where he moved, along with dates and with
full listings of family members. Dedicated church-goers
will leave a good "paper trail" of transfers to mark their
migrations. (For example, Quakers and Baptists are
more likely to have these records of transfers.
Lutherans and Evangelical Reformed usually have
good records of christenings.)

Ask to see donation plaques and lists of con-
tributors to building funds and other projects. These
will give dates and may be in family groups. Lists of
Sunday School teachers (or volunteers for Bible
schools and children's work) may still exist. Women's
groups often leave extensive records of activities that
include many names of the participants. The pastor
may be able to direct you to former pastors still living
who have personal records they have saved. Ask for
their addresses if they no longer live in the area. Ask
for the family of a deceased pastor. They may have his
records stored in an attic and would be willing to share
them with you. Try to find the time to meet older
members of the congregation. One genealogist, arriving

in a small town just as church was dismissed, started talking with the members as they left the building. Their response was very friendly, and she quickly determined that some of them were even her cousins! That may not happen to you, but, by meeting older members of a church, you may share their reminiscences, and perhaps they, too, have records you can use.

Always ask to meet with the current officers of the church. They often have old minutes and group records passed down from one officer to another over the decades. It seems no one ever looks at them, but no one throws them away either. The pastor probably does not realize these records exist since they have no function in current church affairs.

Find out where the members of the church were, and are, being buried. If there is a church cemetery, ask for the records. If the majority of members are buried in a particular secular cemetery, note that is where to start your cemetery research.

Learn if the church was begun as a branch of an established congregation, if it was ever merged with another to form a new congregation, or if it acted as the parent congregation to a new church. Any of these changes could have an effect on where you will find records today.

A reminder—offer to donate a small amount to the church. Most can use the money, and it is a small price to pay for the time they will probably spend helping you.

## CHAPTER 9

# Research in Cemeteries and Funeral Homes

*Now this was a day to remember! Nobody told us how much it can rain here at this time of year, and it's cold, too, out in those cemeteries. Bob wasn't sure which one his ancestors were in so we had to walk around each cemetery for hours looking for tombstones until this nice man came along and told us there was somebody in an office here who had a map that shows where each grave is. (Can you imagine, a map of a cemetery?) Right away we found out where to go, and we were so lucky this was the right cemetery. We couldn't read all the inscriptions, of course, since some were pretty dirty, but we managed to read most of them. It took a little time since they were mixed in with the stones of other people. I don't know why they didn't keep the family together and why they put those strangers in between . . .*

## Dealing with the Living as Well as the Deceased

There is a certain sense of time and of generations past in researching among the records of funeral directors and sextons and in the visiting of cemeteries. Here genealogy, ironically enough, really comes alive for the searcher.

It is usually advisable to check out funeral homes and cemetery associations before going into the cemeteries themselves. Some places will tell you they do not keep records more than a few years old; others have complete files and are almost always pleased to share them. Many records are quite detailed; others are sketchy.

Start by deciding which ones to contact. If you have had the opportunity for advance correspondence with local historians, they will give you guidance. If you are on your own, then Yellow-Page or newspaper ads will often state if a cemetery or funeral home is of a certain age. Funeral homes are generally family affairs and tend to retain their identity for many years. Look for ads that say, "In business since . . ." or "Owned by the fourth generation of our family." If you can identify an ethnic pattern, then take that into consideration in deciding which funeral homes might have dealt with your ancestors. Keep in mind a cooperative funeral director's quick reference to his files may help you locate a cemetery you did not know existed or direct you to the exact place of your family burial. These people, as well as the historical society members, often will have knowledge of obscure private cemeteries as well.

Ask the funeral director who arranged the local burials before his firm existed. There was always some-one performing this service—a local carpenter for the coffin making, a livery stable owner for the horse-drawn hearse, or a stone mason for the marker. Dig as far back as you can for their records. Remember to check local museums and collections for the day books of these businesses. Also ask for the names of other, older funeral homes, so that you can investigate these.

Always ask (beyond the usual questions about date and place of death, burial, etc.) who paid for your ancestor's funeral. Since this was almost always a relative, you may discover maiden surnames, the given names of children, or the name of a son-in-law. Always ask for *everything* in the file.

Ask the funeral director (or sexton in the case of a cemetery) if anyone else has been inquiring about the same burials. Leave some SASE's with them to give to others who might come by later. Be sure to include your surnames with these envelopes.

Praise these people for their preservation of the records and willingness to help you. Encourage sextons by noting how well the cemetery is maintained. (Be particularly lavish with your praise and thanks if you are visiting a privately owned cemetery where your family's graves are on some stranger's land.)

Do not overlook any opportunity to locate cemeteries. Ask the landowner if there are other burials on his property or that of his neighbors. One group of cousins tried in vain to locate a family burial ground. The old hand-drawn maps and directions seemed confusing and did not agree with one another. The family finally found a local farmer working in his fields, and he directed them to a place they had not searched. As they started to go there he asked if they wanted to "see the other one," too. There were *two* cemeteries, a mile apart, reached by separate roads. Both were on the original family land. No wonder the old directions seemed mixed up.

## A Down-to-Earth Approach

Beyond the help you can hope for, and occasionally receive, from others, you must come to the area prepared to conduct your own searches of cemeteries.

The United States Coast and Geodetic Survey maps, county highway department maps, and nineteenth-century atlases are all useful in finding abandoned cemeteries. But be prepared for rough terrain. Even well-maintained cemeteries can require a great deal of walking and some digging around tombstones. Have a list of those ancestors who might be buried in a particular place. (This assumes you have already looked in published records, such as DAR surveys.)

If a cemetery is still being used, check first with the sexton for an index of names. Watch for spelling variations and allied names. Then look at the plot maps. This procedure is very important since the arrangements of graves can be a clue to relationships. If you check only name indexes or look at only your family stones, you miss seeing who is buried in the nearby graves. Be aware that burials were—and still are—usually in family groups. A "strange" name in the middle of a family plot probably has significance and must be investigated. Or consider the situation where a child's grave is among people you cannot identify. Is it possible these are his maternal grandparents and others of their line?

Whether you do this part of your research through sexton's records or by walking through the cemetery, do your search systematically. Have abstract forms to record data (a clip board is handy to give you a firm writing surface outdoors). Make drawings of the grave arrangements so you will have no trouble recalling the exact layout. Record data as you find it, including misspelled names and dates you know are incorrect. Include directions to the grave. (Do not use trees or bushes for this. They can die and be replaced. Instead use some large monument as a guide. For example, "Grandpa's grave is four rows behind the large marble angel on the Smith grave and just to the left when you face the angel.")

There are excellent manuals on cemetery search. These include the identification of the ornate symbolism found on older stones. An understanding of this can help determine the date of the stone and give clues to the deceased. These books also tell you how to photograph stones and make rubbings of the inscriptions. The techniques are too involved to include in this guide, but you should be aware of them if you plan extensive cemetery work.

At the least, take your camera, water, and cloths to clean the stones. A *soft* brush (not a wire one) will loosen dirt without damaging the surface. Talcum powder, shaving cream, even dirt, have all been suggested to highlight inscriptions. There is some disagreement over the advisability of their use. Be careful what you do, take your pictures, and wash the stone afterwards if you can. Foil will act as a good reflector of any light needed for photos, and cardboard can be used to create shadow if that is best for the pictures.

In some cemeteries you may find yourself searching for the stones themselves. Years of neglect and accumulated soil and debris can bury fallen stones. Look for empty pedestals or sunken spots and probe the ground beside them with a tool such as a long screwdriver. A sturdy butcher knife is a good probe also, but be aware of the impression you will make if anyone sees you in an abandoned cemetery "stabbing" graves! Bring trowels or even a small spade to dig out the stone.

Do not forget the unusual way to meet unknown relatives that was suggested earlier. Write down your name, address, phone number with area code, and a statement of your desire to meet your kin. Place the note in a plastic bag and use waterproof tape to attach it to the tombstone. Unless the cemetery is completely abandoned you have a good chance of getting a reply.

Use your research to lead you to other records. Private cemeteries indicate your family probably owned the land at one time, so make the examination of wills, probates, and deeds your next step. Do not overlook having a talk with the current owner of the land. He may be able to tell you something of the history of its ownership and can certainly help you with the legal description you will need to follow through with your investigation. Keep in mind that this is now his land and express your gratitude for his cooperation.

One important suggestion: come prepared for the job. Comfortable shoes, clothes you do not mind getting dirty, garden gloves, a kneeling pad, a sun hat, and bug spray will add to your comfort. Always carry rain gear—coat, hat or scarf, boots—since you probably will not want to miss an opportunity except in real storms. You may want to plan a stop at a service station or restaurant bathroom after your cemetery work to change clothes and wash off some of the dirt or mud.

The final suggestion is one that you may not appreciate the importance of until you try it. Sit down in the cemetery and just look around. Somehow, in the open space, you will catch an idea of your family's place in this land. Especially in a private cemetery, there is a feeling of these people actually being there. They probably knew these trees as saplings and may have planted the hedges or sown the flower seeds. Make this a time to appreciate their lives and contribution to your heritage. Step back and take one last photograph to remind you of the way the land looked and felt.

# Newspapers as a Resource

*Would you believe the newspapers here don't keep files of their own paper? Said they keep them in the state archives. We did find some microfilmed ones in the library, but Bob got such a headache reading them I had to take over, and when I left my purse on the floor to get a drink of water, somebody took it. I didn't know there were thieves in libraries. It's a good thing I was wearing my glasses. I don't know what I'd do without them. I only wish I'd gotten my prescription changed before I started out on this trip . . .*

## Local Collections and Files

Your preparation at home should have made you aware of where old newspapers are collected, so you probably already realize they are not necessarily in the places you expect. Your own librarian will have helped you use the specialized reference books that give you the names and publication dates of defunct papers and where they may be found. It is very likely worth the effort to travel where these collections are housed and spend time searching them in detail.

Whether you do this searching in a central archive or library or in your ancestors' home town, the procedure is very much the same, and its success depends both on your knowledge of your family's presence in the area during particular time periods and on your willingness to do the job thoroughly. Newspaper research can be both time consuming and profitable. It requires concentration.

Start by asking if these are the only papers. The archivist may know of others that somehow do not appear in the reference book. Ask about ethnic papers also. Do not overlook regional publications that might include news from the community you are interested in. Also, be aware that articles may appear in more than one newspaper.

Ask if there are any indexes. Some genealogical libraries are now doing surname indexes to their local newspaper files. These are not usually comprehensive but may help in your work. Some reference centers have indexed feature articles. Check these for anything related to your family.

A few papers publish a summary of births, marriages, and deaths in the first issue of a new year. This is an easy way to direct yourself to family references.

Using your family group sheets and other records as your guide to dates, read issues of the paper several weeks before and after the event you are interested in. Newspapers may make reference to a wedding in advance of the date or have a follow-up article later. It might be some time before a birth or death was reported (and in many cases these were not ever published), so check an extended time period and look for more than one article. Remember coverage was often incomplete and delayed.

Placement of articles was often at random. Deaths and funeral notices were scattered throughout the text so it is wise to read all of a small newspaper. The larger papers present a problem. Learn to scan and identify articles quickly. But be aware that even an item on a national subject may have a local reference. There may be mention of community leaders; quotations from business men, pastors, and teachers; and accounts of local problems as part of the national situation. Allow time for the careful reading you will need to do.

What can you expect from newspapers? Think what occupies your own life. Remember that papers, then as now, are always hungry for material and anxious to please subscribers. People like to read about others in their community. Look for coverage of the following:

- Special events—births, christenings, marriages, deaths, graduations, and anniversaries.

- Business news—opening of new businesses, closing of factories, announcements of new officers, farm problems. (Keep in mind that economic conditions were a powerful factor in migration. The report of an extended drought could be your clue to why great-grandpa moved on West.)

- Parties—these were often recorded in great detail, including guest lists that mentioned relationships and home towns.

- Organizations—the formation of new women's groups, businessmen's associations, veteran's organizations, churches. The reports will indicate the names of members and personal details.

- Civic affairs—including any political activity. Look for road and building dedications, campaigns and elections, local celebrations.

- Personal activities—travel was long considered a novelty and papers gave details of trips that contain genealogical clues. For

example, "Mrs. Smith just returned from visiting her sister at the family home in
Lynchburg, Virginia. She was pleased to see
the old place and know it is being kept up
since it has been in her family from the 1850s
when her father, the Reverend Samuel Smith,
came from Devon, England, to establish a
Presbyterian church."

■  Court actions—adoptions, settlements of land
disputes (excellent for guiding you to deeds
and other records), civil and criminal cases.

■  Military service—accounts of battles and
casualties; of those who were drafted, enlisted, or discharged; of memorials and com-
memorative events.

■  Schools and colleges—faculty, students', and
supporters' names all can appear in
newspaper accounts.

The wealth of detail will surprise you. Relationships and dates are often given. People are described
as "formally of . . ." and "moving to . . ." Women are
referred to as "the former Miss . . ." and men as "the
son of . . ." Often there is much more information given
in older papers than is found in modern papers.

Be especially alert for reunion and community
anniversary accounts. These are more common than
you realize and almost always list the participants and
give historic details. They may involve family groups,
alumni, old settlers, and veterans. A colorful example
is the extensive file in a collection in Missouri contain-
ing newspaper accounts of the border raiders who rode
with Quantrill. Their reunions took place over many
years and were given in-depth coverage by the local
papers each time.

Do not overlook the ads—both business and individual; they can offer genealogical clues. You may

find your ancestor's home advertised, stating he has "been at the same location for thirty years," or that he is "Going West. Must sell everything."

Use the information you find to enlarge your search. When you encounter "formally lived in . . ." then look at the newspapers of that community for family members and activities, obituaries, and other genealogical data. See the papers as a chain of clues stretching back in time.

If you are not having luck in your search, then look at the papers of surrounding communities. There were often overlapping areas of reporting, and an event may have taken place in a different town. One researcher tried in vain to locate a marriage record in the town the family lived in. When she widened her search she found the couple was married many miles away even though they had obtained their license at home. Check outlying papers to avoid missing such events.

The obituaries of siblings and of friends of the family are important to check. Neighbors and friends serve as pallbearers at funerals so look for your family names in the death notices of people you really do not know (or you may recognize them from census records as neighbors of your family).

Watch out for persons of the same name as your ancestor. It might be a coincidence, or it might be a cousin. Do not be confused and assume someone is your ancestor because he has the same name and spells it the same way. Check other sources before you reach a conclusion.

There are often deliberate errors in newspaper accounts. Women sometimes listed themselves as being a few years younger, especially when they knew the information would be published for the community to read. Old people might have exaggerated their age as a matter of pride or bragged about being active at a particular time when they were really born after the historic event.

Colorful reporting was the commonly accepted practice. Activities were often described in terms more appropriate to novels than the modern-day newspaper. Editorializing within the reporting was common also. The publisher of the paper saw no reason to withhold his opinion, even in a news article.

Be sure to *enjoy* the newspapers as you look for your genealogical data. Try to see them as your ancestors did when they read the latest edition. If you can somehow drop the perspective your knowledge of history gives you, then for a brief moment you can imagine what it was like to live in a particular time and read that day's news without having any idea of the outcome of the stories being reported. Take time to consider the effect each issue of the paper would have had on your family members and their understanding of the world around them.

## The Personal Memories and Experiences of Feature Writers and Journalists

When you are in a community, even if you have used newspaper files elsewhere, stop at the office of the currently published paper. Remember, you are interrupting their work, so be brief and considerate. If you can read copies of the paper first, learn the names of editors and feature writers you might want to meet.

Start by praising their fine work and their service to the community. Mention a particular feature article or a column on local history. Try to talk with the writer if you can. These people are walking files of information on the history itself and on where to research. Learn what sources they used. Ask them about historic sites, famous people, and events, and gradually start referring to your own family and its presence in the area. Offer to take them out to lunch. (Remember the courthouse clerks? Writers get hungry too.)

If the writer is cooperative and you feel there may be more to learn, ask if anyone else writes about local history or if anyone used to write for the paper and retired. Be friendly but persistent. Only a fraction of the data gathered by a writer is ever printed. With luck you can acquire some of this knowledge and use it in your own research.

# Do Not Forget
# the Unusual Sources

*We spent all day trying to find the home Bob's great-grandparents
built. He thought it was on the east side of town, but he couldn't find
the address in his files. That section is mostly freeway and a
shopping center, anyway, so we gave up. I knew there must be some
way to locate it, so we went to the library here and guess what? The
census records give addresses! (I thought they only gave names and
ages.) And you know, we found it right there, behind a convenience
store. It's being used as a storage shed, I think. Bob was pretty
disappointed. His mother had told him it was two stories, brick with
columns in front, and had a big veranda. I guess that just shows
you how wrong those family stories can be . . .*

## Searching for Unique Possibilities

Too often we think only of vital records, land
records, property documents, and the more legal, formal data left behind by our ancestors. We overlook the
subtle everyday evidence of their lives. As you did in
your research in newspapers, consider now what activities and interests your ancestors may have been
involved with — what kind of lives they led. Analyze your

family traditions. What do they tell your great-grandfather was doing? Look at your family heirlooms. What do they tell you about great-grandmother's interests? Once more, think of what occupies *your life* and then imagine what they might have been doing.

Does the home town have hobby and special interest groups that have been in existence for some time? Could your ancestors have been part of these? Wood carvings, quilts, and crafts of many kinds have been popular over the years. Have these groups, even if more recently organized, preserved records of older groups or saved their handiwork? Have clubs been built around occupations? Retired railroad workers and others have collections of memorabilia that include names and lists of people and their activities. Professional people establish museums and display the artifacts from their occupations (such as medicine, dentistry, etc.).

A visit to local schools and colleges can be more productive than you might imagine. Some public schools are becoming aware of genealogical interest and are allowing their enrollment records to be published, subject to privacy laws. But a great deal of material is there for you to find only through a personal search. Start with the administrator to gain his approval and direction. Ask where the records are kept and how to access them. Make sure he understands your interest is only in very old records. See if there are defunct schools whose records are in storage separately from others. Your advance study of census surveys should allow you to narrow your search to specific schools by checking the addresses of your family residences against school district maps.

Investigate parochial schools where that is appropriate to your family background. But do not overlook the possibility that Protestant children might attend a Catholic school or that a Catholic might be in a public one.

Use class records to learn names of parents and the given names of siblings and to confirm ages and dates. Depending on the district's records there may be considerable extra family and health information available to you.

Local colleges will usually be cooperative and can tell you a great deal about your ancestors. Be sure to ask for alumni records as well, since these contain accounts of employment, marriage, children, and changes of residence.

Fraternal organizations are often quite welcoming to genealogists. Ask when the local unit was formed, what records are kept there, and what has been sent to a central office. If you can, talk to some of the members to see if any have old record books or organizational material.

Using your knowledge of your ancestors' background, investigate the political clubs in which you think he might have participated. County histories and newspapers may already have given you membership lists, but the clubs may have more information on former members. At the least, you may find out the kind of political events with which your great-grandfather was concerned.

Labor unions and business organizations may have detailed records kept over a long period of time. Places of employment, education, insurance, and lists of family members may all be recorded, as are changes of address and changes of status such as illness, marriage, births of children, and deaths.

Military posts have museums and, in connection with these, much general historical and genealogical information aside from their official records, which are usually in a central records archives. Curators are usually older soldiers, eager and willing to discuss your ancestor's period of service.

Veterans' organizations, like the military itself, keep detailed records that are generally quite helpful.

Do not forget those for more distant wars, such as the Grand Army of the Republic (GAR) and the United Daughters of the Confederacy (UDC), which preserve wonderful details of Civil War times.

By thinking of the period in which your female ancestors lived and their ages during this time, you may be able to locate women's groups that have preserved records, if not of your specific ancestor, at least of the era in which she was active. Suffragette and temperance movements, literary societies, tea and luncheon groups, civic health and improvement societies, and auxiliaries to men's organizations are all possible groups that may have modern "descendants" who have preserved the old records themselves or have given them to collections. Ask YWCA staff and members about older community groups and check modern women's clubs for older members who know of early women's activities. Some original groups may simply have changed name and purpose and continue to exist.

As we stressed earlier, do not fail to visit with local members of hereditary societies to learn of information not held by their national headquarters.

It may seem strange to suggest hospital records as a possible genealogical source because of the confidentiality involved, but there are some unusual records open to the public. An interesting example is in a hospital that keeps a "birth book" listing each baby as it is born. The volume, on display to the public, goes through several generations already.

If you can find a realtor who has a little time and a love of history, you can get valuable information on the growth of the community and its pattern of housing and development. Again, this is not specific genealogical data but it may help you understand your family.

Finally, do not forget to look for the houses once occupied by your ancestors. Most will probably be gone, but some will still exist, and even seeing the house lots and the general neighborhood will be of interest. Look also for commercial buildings that may have had a part in your ancestors' lives.

Use rotary clubs, chambers of commerce, and tourist bureaus to locate a wide variety of groups and individuals that may lead you to unusual genealogical finds.

# When You Are Not Alone: Special Considerations for Group Travel

*What a strange experience we had yesterday. Someone told Bob the local genealogy group was taking an all-day bus trip to the state archives. Well, we hadn't been there yet so this sounded like a good way to go. It was really fun. I know we had a good time, just talking all the way. A few people were very unsociable, of course. I never understand people who keep their noses in their books all the time. One woman even asked us to be quiet, but Bob really settled that when he told her he had paid just as much as she and had a right to talk. Anyway it was fun, even if we didn't find anything in the files. Those things are really hard to use unless you study beforehand . . .*

## Genealogical Packages

Occasionally, you will have the opportunity to take a trip with other genealogists. These trips are usually planned to visit specific libraries and research centers and are advertised through genealogical and historical societies. There are many things to consider before you decide on this approach to research.

## Advantages

It is almost always less expensive than traveling on your own.

You will travel directly to the places where you want to study. There will be no hunt for a parking space, no taxi from your hotel. You will be let off and picked up at the door of the facility.

There will be someone to take care of your luggage. All you have to do is be sure it is ready on time each morning. There is no handling of heavy luggage or tipping porters.

Your motels and meals will be reserved and arranged. If there is a problem, you will not have to deal with it.

When you get to the research centers you will be met by someone in authority and given guidance in finding your way through the collection.

You will be given lectures en route to each new library so you will arrive familiar with what you are about to see.

Your companions will be knowledgeable. They will constantly exchange information with you and with each other and often will offer help with your research problems.

Moreover, these companions will understand and sympathize with what you are doing. They will not demand to stop at tourist attractions and cause you to lose time in research. They will share your interests.

## Disadvantages

You will have to follow the itinerary and the rules. You cannot choose your lodging or your restaurants. Hours will be fixed.

You will be limited in your luggage and, therefore, in the genealogical material you can take along.

There will be no side trips to your family's own historic sites, such as cemeteries, homes, or churches. There may be no chance to go off on your own.

If you make a wonderful discovery in your research, you will not be able to change your plans to take advantage of it by staying longer in one place or going on to another courthouse. You will have to go where the group goes.

Some of your companions may have come along only for the social experience. You may be tempted to spend time talking rather than researching. If you are easily distracted from work this can be a problem.

A distinct disadvantage is that a group trip runs the risk of being cancelled because of poor enrollment. Often there is a delay in getting a refund of your deposit, and always there is a sense of disappointment when you have prepared for your adventure and then cannot take the trip.

## Questions to Ask
## before You Decide

Ask around to find out how others feel about trips they have taken with the same organizer. Is the sponsor reliable? Were the accommodations and plans as advertised? Were they comfortable? Was there adequate instruction and were the lectures given by experienced people?

Find out in *writing* about costs and who pays for what. Are *all* meals included? Are tips expected?

Exactly what luggage can you take?

Is the schedule relaxed enough to allow for frequent stops, adequate rest, and recreation?

Is there provision for some sightseeing and relaxation?

What is the smoking/nonsmoking policy?

What is the extra charge for rooming alone? The

presence of a roommate may be a pleasant social experience, and you may make a new friend. You certainly can exchange genealogical tips and share your ideas of the day's experiences, but consider also the advantage of not having to share a bathroom and having time alone each day to review your data. Only you can decide if you want to be in this close proximity to a stranger for a prolonged time. It could be the best—or worst—week of your life.

Do not fail to get in writing the policy on cancellation and refunds. What if you become ill before the trip? During the trip? If there is a family emergency? If there is not adequate enrollment? Check dates for cancellation notices and refunds.

Approach the trip as a business contract as well as a genealogical opportunity and you will be well prepared for a group experience.

## CHAPTER 13

# *Back at Home*

*We came back home yesterday. What a relief! At last we can talk about something besides genealogy. I'm sorry Bob didn't find what he was looking for, but maybe we can go there again in a few years. I wish we'd taken down the addresses of some of those people we met. It might be nice to write them and see how they are doing on their research. Right now we're both too tired to write any letters to anybody. Bob just took those boxes we carried around with us and put them on the shelves downstairs. He said he doesn't want to see any charts or forms for six months. I think he's upset because we lost that file with his grandmother's diary. We probably shouldn't have taken it on the trip, but we didn't have time to make a copy. Maybe someone will find it, but I don't think we put our name on the box. Oh well. Bob says we need to plan on going to the genealogical society meeting this weekend. He wants to give a report to the others. He thinks maybe we could get some of them interested in going on a trip together. Since we've had experience now, it should be easy to do . . .*

## Laying a Basis for the Future

When you return home the worst thing you can do is to put your papers away, rest, and catch up on household and business affairs without following up on your research trip. There are many things you should be doing as soon as possible after you get home and others you can continue to do in the months ahead.

## Minding Your Manners: The Importance of Saying "Thank You"

Manners are important in genealogy just as they are in other aspects of life. When people help us in some way, it is our responsibility to let them know what their help meant to us and that we appreciate it.

Writing a note or sending a small gift, if possible, will show you are grateful and it will, in the case of public officials, remind them that genealogists are people with sensitivity and feelings. You may be smoothing the way for the next genealogist to visit a clerk's office.

Whenever it is advisable, send genealogical information also. Relatives will want to see copies of the new information you discovered on your trip or receive copies of documents you told them you had. Local genealogists and historians may want copies for their own collections. Be generous. The more data you distribute the greater the chances of receiving future help. Always enclose an SASE to encourage the exchange of papers in the future.

At intervals in the future, continue to send short follow-up notes as a reminder of you and of your interest. Tell people of any new discoveries you make, send copies of information, and, in general, make every effort to continue your relationship without becoming a nuisance. (Be sure to include a new SASE whenever one is used in reply to you.)

Do not forget to send your new findings and copies of your summaries to other family researchers with whom you are in touch. They will be just as interested in your discoveries as the people you visited.

## Filing and Evaluating Your Discoveries

Remember the basic rule given earlier: good research deserves further study under better conditions. Apply in reverse the principle of preparation you used for your trip. This time, devote two hours of review for every research hour you spent while traveling.

It is important that you make this review right away while the material is still fresh in your mind. There may be clarification needed in your notes, and you should do this before your memory is dulled by time and the pressure of outside commitments.

Once you are satisfied your new material is complete and clearly recorded, then integrate it into your files. Be sure the new papers all give the source and date of your work. As you file, compare the new and old information. Look for inconsistencies and clues and make note of these.

Write a summary of what you now *know* about a particular segment of your genealogy. Then write a summary of what you *think* about that line.

Using the summaries as a basis, write an outline for your future research. Decide what can be accomplished through local libraries, inquiries by mail, and other sources you can use while still at home. You may also decide to hire someone in the area to which you traveled to do further research there on material you did not have time to examine or on speculations that occurred to you after you left. Your review of your work at home will help you pinpoint where this assistance would be most valuable, and the contacts you make on this trip will help you employ a competent researcher.

Once you have finished dealing with your genealogical materials, take time to write a brief outline of your search and travel information. This will be of use to you if you go into the area again and will give you something concrete to share with fellow genealogists who may go there later and ask you for advice. Include names of motels and restaurants, warnings about bad roads, and comments on the availability of information in courthouses. Write down reminders of ways to make a trip easier or things to avoid in future travels.

Send any new surnames you found to the genealogical societies to which you belong, in order to keep your records current and, perhaps, to find local connections with your surname. If you can, consider writing articles for your societies' publications. By sharing details of your trip and your research you will be helping others and yourself.

## Planning Your Next Trip

By writing your research and travel summaries you will be well on your way to planning your next trip. Use the clues you now have to pinpoint your area of search. Try not to skip around geographically. Concentration on searching for a particular line in a particular area will give focus to your work. Be especially alert for "blank spots" in the migration pattern and try to fill these in before you go on to a new area.

If it does happen you have not been successful in finding your ancestor's records, try working in a circle around the area you searched. They may have been living just outside the section where you have been looking. Learn more about the geography and history of the area to determine what might have caused them to settle elsewhere, and be prepared to start searching in that place next time. Do not be discouraged. There is a basic satisfaction in knowing you attempted something difficult. As one archivist said, "You can't find something that isn't there." It may be somewhere else, just waiting for you to find it on your next trip.

# A Final Word

## What Constitutes
## a Successful Trip

Any trip, no matter how limited, should increase your knowledge of your family's personal history. Unless your ancestors hid themselves completely, you will find records of some kind—bits and pieces to add to your genealogical puzzle. These are the pieces you could not have discovered by staying at home.

Beyond this specific genealogical data is another benefit only a trip can bring. You should return with a larger understanding of your family's background. Dates and events will gain meaning when you really see where your people lived. It is an experience of your past you cannot get from correspondence or library research, no matter how thorough, because it is based on the area itself.

A good trip will reveal truths about your family to you. It will make you confront the past with honesty and with awareness of the character of your ancestors, including their sins and indiscretions as well as their virtues. You will be meeting *them* not just their statistics.

Finally, a successful trip will give you a sense of direction for further study. It will eliminate areas of search, provide clues, help you to begin work on previously unknown lines, and define new goals in your work. It will act as the stimulus as well as the basis for your future genealogical activity.

## Is a Research Trip a Vacation?

Certainly a research trip should be fun. The traveler who leaves home with an attitude of grim determination is missing the whole spirit of genealogy. Like a vacation, this trip should be a pleasant experience, a break from everyday life.

But also like a vacation it needs planning. On a vacation you must be aware of what you want to see and do. A haphazard approach can cause you to miss visiting places you would like to see or participating in activities you had wanted to experience. Arriving after the close of a county courthouse is like getting to Disneyland after the rides have shut down. You either have to wait until the next day or go somewhere else and lose the chance completely. It is better to plan ahead and know just when that courthouse is open.

Like a vacation, your trip will benefit from information you can gather at home. Just as it is better to read the guidebook in advance rather than at the vacation site, so it is better to understand just what you will be seeing on a research trip. Imagine standing in the Tower of London and not knowing anything about British history. Think of what you would miss! Now imagine doing the same thing in genealogy—passing through a Civil War battlefield without knowing exactly what occurred there, only knowing that your great-grandfather fought there once. Or think of driving through the Cumberland Gap frontier and not understanding the significance of the geography.

Any trip is more pleasant when you satisfy the necessities of travel without wasting time and without irritation. Remember vacations where you spent hours looking for a motel or did not get a decent meal for three days? That frustration can affect research trips as well. Avoiding it can give you extra time to study and save your energy for more important things like finding whole new generations of ancestors. Remember, too, that a research trip, like a vacation, should be satisfying for all its participants. A spouse who is really not involved in genealogy may become an asset if he or she is included in the planning and given an understanding of what can be expected on the trip. Providing for non-genealogical activities that appeal to him or her is important and will pay off in assistance as well as companionship in the long run.

Any vacation may require skills—skiing, swimming, etc.—and a genealogical trip is no different. You would not go diving without scuba instruction or hiking without knowing what to carry in your backpack. Treat your research in the same way. Learning to survey a cemetery or to use a library properly is a vital part of your preparation.

Of course, there are differences between a vacation and a research trip. Vacations are usually in areas that have adapted to visits by tourists. On a genealogy trip you may be in small towns that have little need for visitor accommodations. Motels may be few and restaurants may be limited. Just keeping in mind that the purpose of your trip is knowledge, not a four-star meal, will help you accept less than ideal conditions.

A research trip may contain more disappointments and frustration than a vacation. (Although some vacations can be disastrous themselves!) Since you are trying to reach goals that may not be attainable, you must keep your perspective and still enjoy the experience.

There may be more necessity to change plans on a research trip. A new clue may send you to a different county than one you had planned to search or the discovery of an abandoned cemetery may cause you to spend an extra day in a particular location. This flexibility should be expected and allowed for in your planning.

Ideally your trip should be a balance of research and vacation. The research should be fun and the vacation should be educational. Satisfying your search for adventure by hunting for ancestors may be better than any safari taken in Africa or as thrilling as any ride in Disneyland.

# *A Reminder of Things to Do*

## Chapter 1

- ☐ Determine your area of search.
- ☐ Study local geography.
- ☐ Study local history.
- ☐ Study tourist information.
- ☐ Analyze your files.
- ☐ Update your files.
- ☐ Be sure you have all census data recorded.
- ☐ Study legal procedures and terms.
- ☐ Learn about calendar changes.
- ☐ Learn about handwriting.
- ☐ Study library research techniques.
- ☐ Talk with knowledgeable people at home.
- ☐ Write to libraries and research centers.
- ☐ Check for surnames in the area.
- ☐ Subscribe to local newspapers.

☐ Make inquiries of local newspapers.

☐ Establish contacts with knowledgeable people in the area.

## Chapter 2

☐ Check research center hours and rules.

☐ Check road conditions.

☐ Organize your travel research files.

☐ Make copies of papers to take with you.

☐ Identify all copies of papers.

☐ Take maps and vacation guides.

☐ Take membership cards and identification.

☐ Take library and research tools.

☐ Take glasses, medications, and health aids.

☐ Take state research guides and glossaries.

☐ Take copies of family photos.

☐ Take cemetery search tools.

## Chapter 3

☐ Make motel reservations.

☐ Plan and adjust your daily schedule according to need.

☐ Eat healthy meals.

☐ Take time to rest and exercise.

☐ Wear comfortable clothes, especially shoes.

☐ Keep your filing system current with your research.

☐ Copy legibly.

☐ Review your work frequently.

## Chapter 4

- ☐ Exchange information with relatives in advance.
- ☐ Arrange visits.
- ☐ Compare photos.
- ☐ Use bulletin boards and newsletters for contacts.
- ☐ Appeal to local people for help.

## Chapter 5

- ☐ Become knowledgeable about individual libraries.
- ☐ Allow time to get acquainted with each library.
- ☐ Enlist a local person to assist you.
- ☐ Look for special holdings and unique material.
- ☐ Have a search plan and an alternate plan.
- ☐ Make any reservations necessary.

## Chapter 6

- ☐ Visit and establish friendships with local people.
- ☐ Identify local groups.
- ☐ Look for local museums and collections.

## Chapter 7

- ☐ Present a professional appearance.
- ☐ Know what you want and what you are likely to find.

☐ Look for unknown records.

☐ Be aware of clues to relationships.

☐ Leave a SASE.

☐ Be friendly.

## Chapter 8

☐ Determine the church denomination.

☐ Study church history and structure.

☐ Contact a variety of people for records.

## Chapter 9

☐ Use funeral directors to locate cemeteries.

☐ Be aware of grave-site patterns.

☐ Be prepared for work.

☐ Use family cemeteries to find land records.

## Chapter 10

☐ Locate newspaper files, including ethnic papers.

☐ Check indexes.

☐ Read thoroughly.

☐ Contact local writers.

☐ Identify sources used by local writers.

## Chapter 11

☐ Locate and contact organizations and groups.

## Chapter 12

☐ Get travel policies in writing.

☐ Ask basic questions before you sign up.

☐ Make decisions based on your personal needs.

## Chapter 13

☐ Send notes of appreciation.

☐ Send copies of new information to other researchers.

☐ Review your work.

☐ Integrate the new material into your files.

☐ Write a summary of what you *know* and *think.*

☐ Write an outline for future research.

☐ Follow up on clues.

☐ Write an outline of your travel information.

☐ Send new surnames to your genealogical societies.

☐ Write an article for your genealogical societies.

☐ Decide on the area for your next trip.

## Research Methodology

Cerny, Johni and Arlene H. Eakle. *Ancestry's Guide to Research: Case Studies in American Genealogy.* Salt Lake City, Utah: Ancestry, 1984. Excellent guide to the research process. A how-to book illustrated by case histories.

Greenwood, Val D. *The Researcher's Guide to American Genealogy.* 1973. 2d ed. Baltimore, Md.: Genealogical Publishing Co., 1990. A textbook of genealogy. Especially good for directing the researcher to land records and their analysis.

Linder, Bill R. *How to Trace Your Family History: A Basic Guide to Genealogy.* New York, N.Y.: Everest House, 1978. Clear, concise how-to information.

## Reference Books and Directories

Bentley, Elizabeth. *County Courthouse Book.* Baltimore, Md.: Genealogical Publishing Company, 1990.

Eakle, Arlene and Johni Cerny, eds. *The Source: A Guidebook of American Genealogy.* Salt Lake City, Utah: Ancestry, 1984. The single most comprehensive reference book available. Individual chapters should be consulted for in-depth directories and extensive bibliographies for a variety of resources. The sections of particular interest to the genealogical traveler are those on lineage societies, land and court records, churches, cemeteries, newspapers, ethnic groups, urban research, business and institutional research, and military records.

Eichholz, Alice, ed. *Ancestry's Red Book: American State, County & Town Sources.* 1989. Revised. Salt Lake City, Utah: Ancestry, 1992. Gives fingertip access to the holdings of each county in the United States. Features include earliest land, probate, birth, marriage, death, and court record dates for every county; also, current addresses, formation date, parent county listings, and maps. In-depth discussions on research in each state are presented.

*The Handybook for Genealogists.* 1947. Revised. Logan, Utah: Everton Publishers, 1991. Now in its eighth edition, this reference has included (with its traditional listings such as vital, land, property, and court records) a section on migration routes and a comprehensive list of archives, genealogical libraries, and societies for each state.

Meitzler, Leland. *United States County Courthouse Address Book.* Orting, Wash.: Heritage Quest, 1988.

Meyer, Mary K. *Meyer's Directory of Genealogical Societies in the USA and Canada.* 1990. Contains listings of genealogical, special interest and state societies, umbrella groups, one-name family organizations, and periodicals.

## Specialized References

Eakle, Arlene H. *Photograph Analysis.* Salt Lake City, Utah: Family History World, 1976. A book that will help greatly in understanding the importance of family photographs.

Evans, Barbara Jean. *A to ZAX: A Glossary of Terminology for Genealogists and Social Historians.* Utica, Ky.: McDowell Publishing, 1983. Extensive entries. A good reference for use when searching records using legal, technical, and archaic terms.

Frisch-Ripley, Karen. *Unlocking the Secrets in Old Photographs.* Salt Lake City, Utah: Ancestry, 1991. Includes sections on identifying the family, dating photographs, recognizing types of photographs, and care and restoration.

Harris, Maurine and Glen, comps. *Ancestry's Concise Genealogical Dictionary.* Salt Lake City, Utah: Ancestry, 1989.

Kirkham, E. Kay. *The Handwriting of American Records for a Period of 300 Years.* Logan, Utah: Everton Publishers, 1973. Basic instruction on handwriting interpretation. A valuable aid for deciphering old records.

Mann, Thomas. *A Guide to Library Research Methods.* New York, N.Y.: Oxford University Press, 1987. A solid approach to library use. A manual of search methods for the modern library facility.

Shull, Wilma Sadler. *Photographing Your Heritage.* Salt Lake City, Utah: Ancestry, 1988. Includes sections on photographing documents, gravestones, and heirlooms.

Sturm, Duane and Pat. *Video Family History.* Salt Lake City, Utah: Ancestry, 1989. Techniques and demonstrations are presented here in nontechnical language for producing a unique family heirloom.

## Area-Specific References

The reader should be aware of the various state guides available and the specialized publications dealing with regions or historical periods. Consult the following for in-depth listings:

Filby, P. William, comp. *American & British Genealogy & Heraldry: A Selected List of Books.* Boston, Mass.: New England Historic Genealogical Society, 1983.

Schreiner-Yantis, Netti, comp. *Genealogical Books in Print.* 1985. Springfield, Va.: Genealogical Books in Print, 1990.